Se

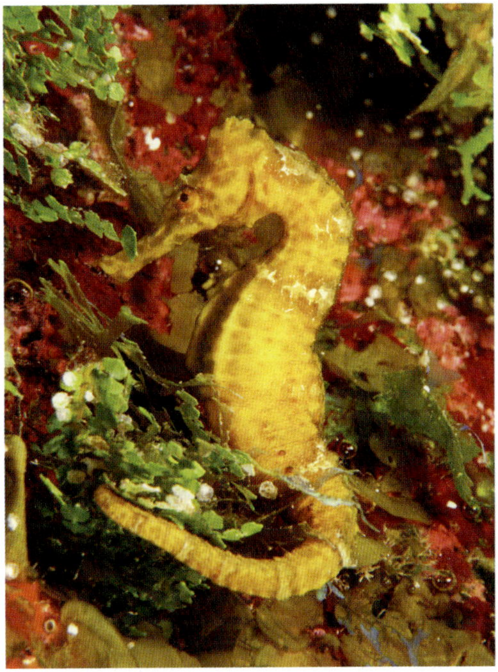

written by Pam Holden

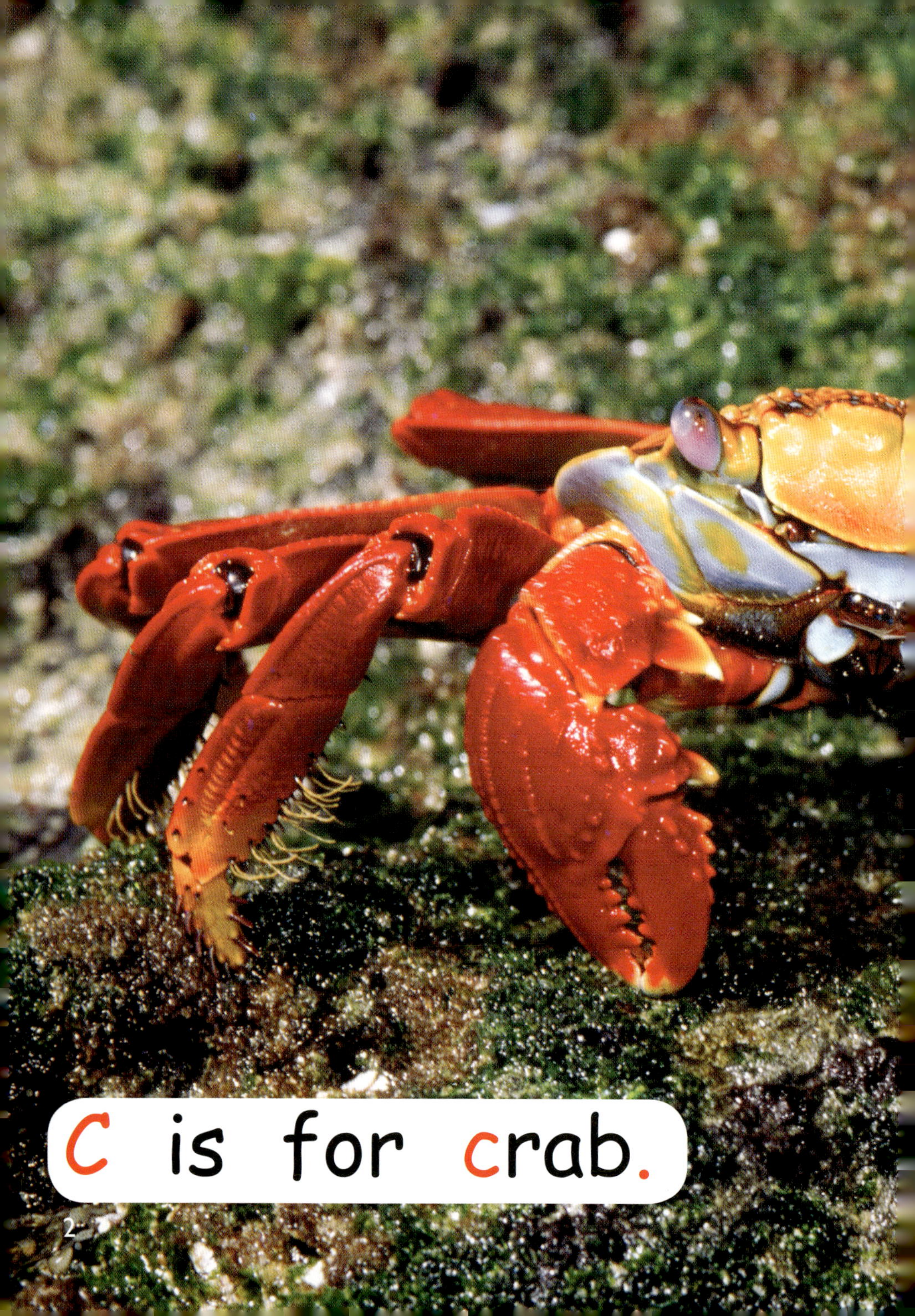

C is for crab.

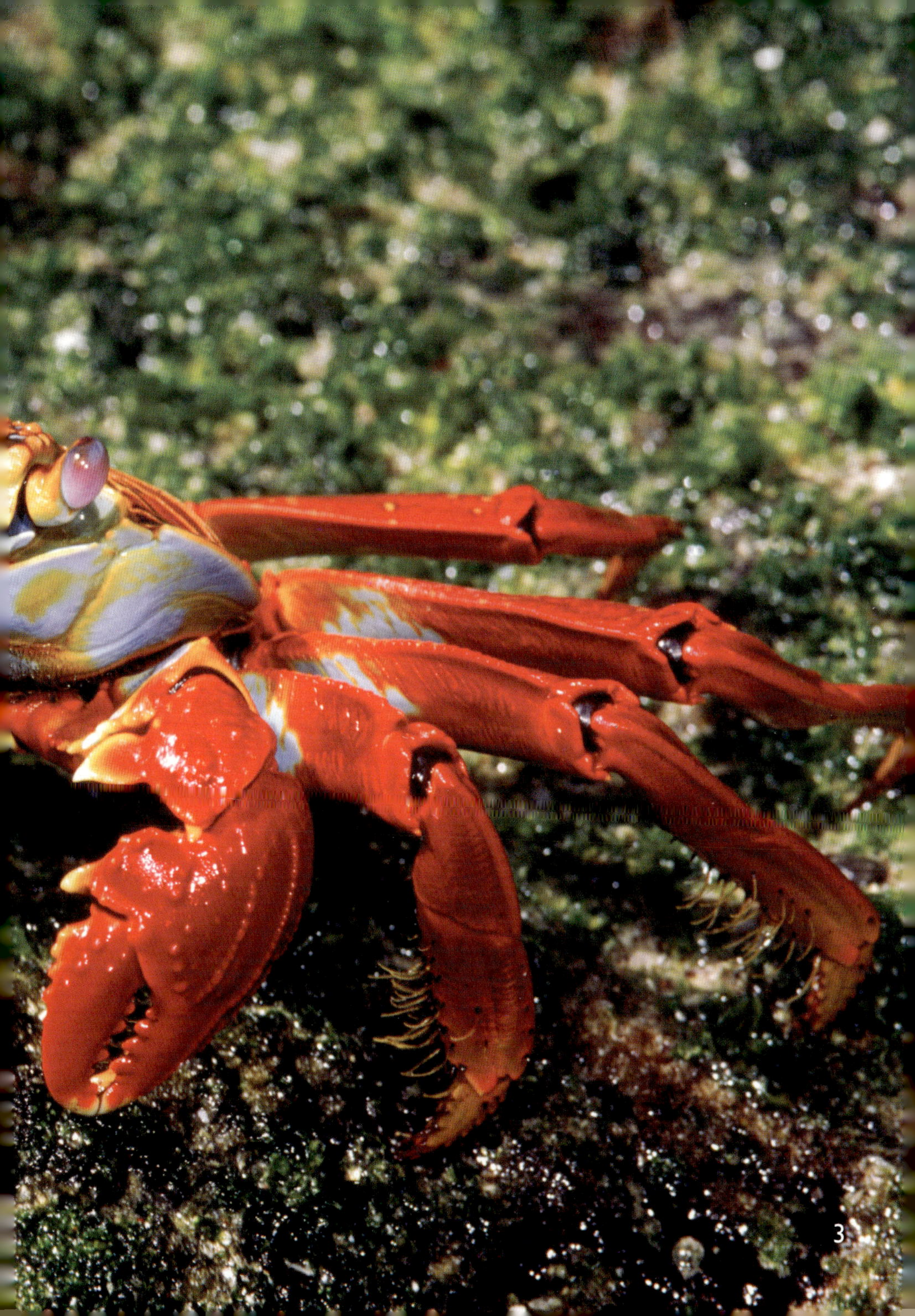

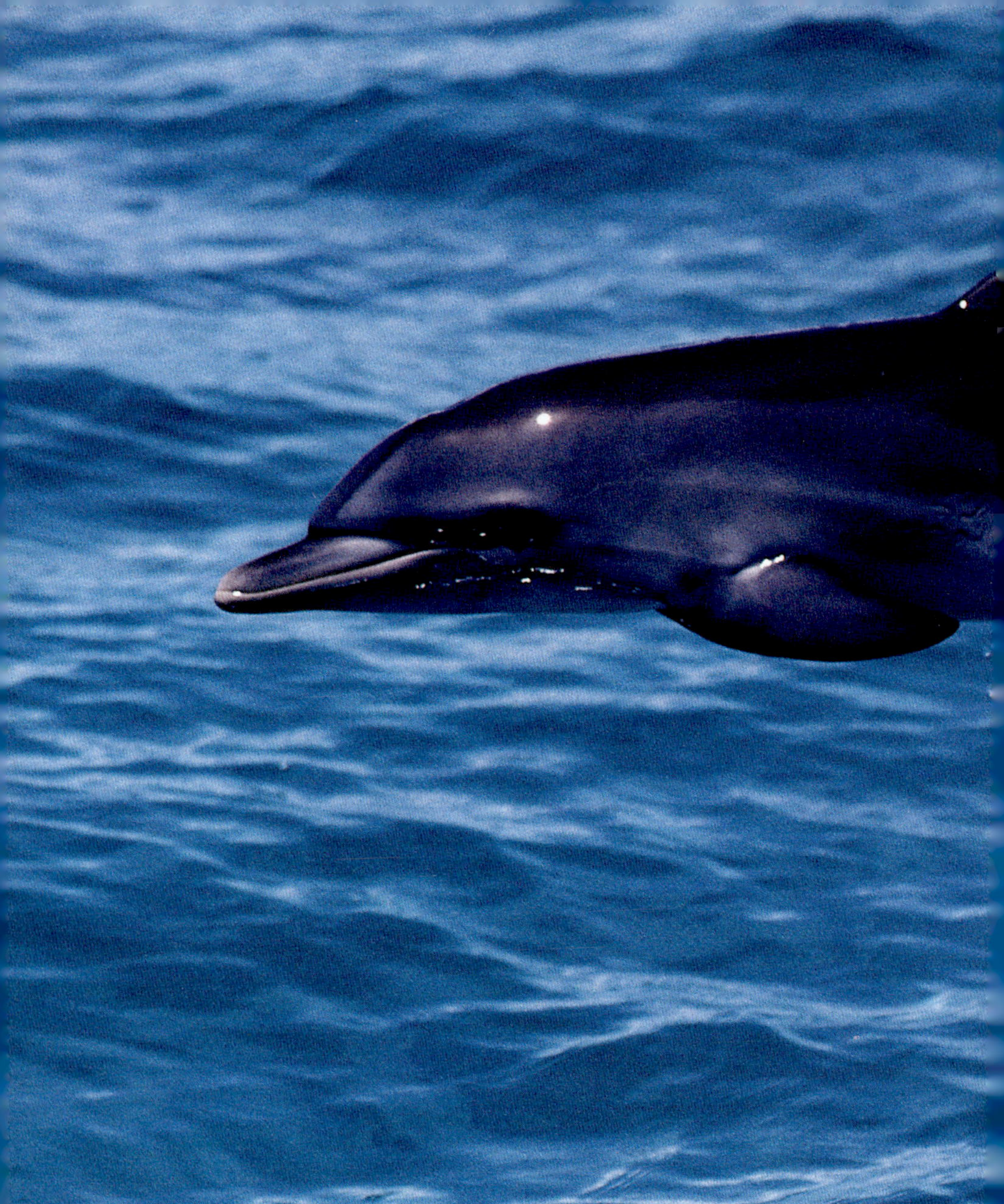

D is for dolphin.

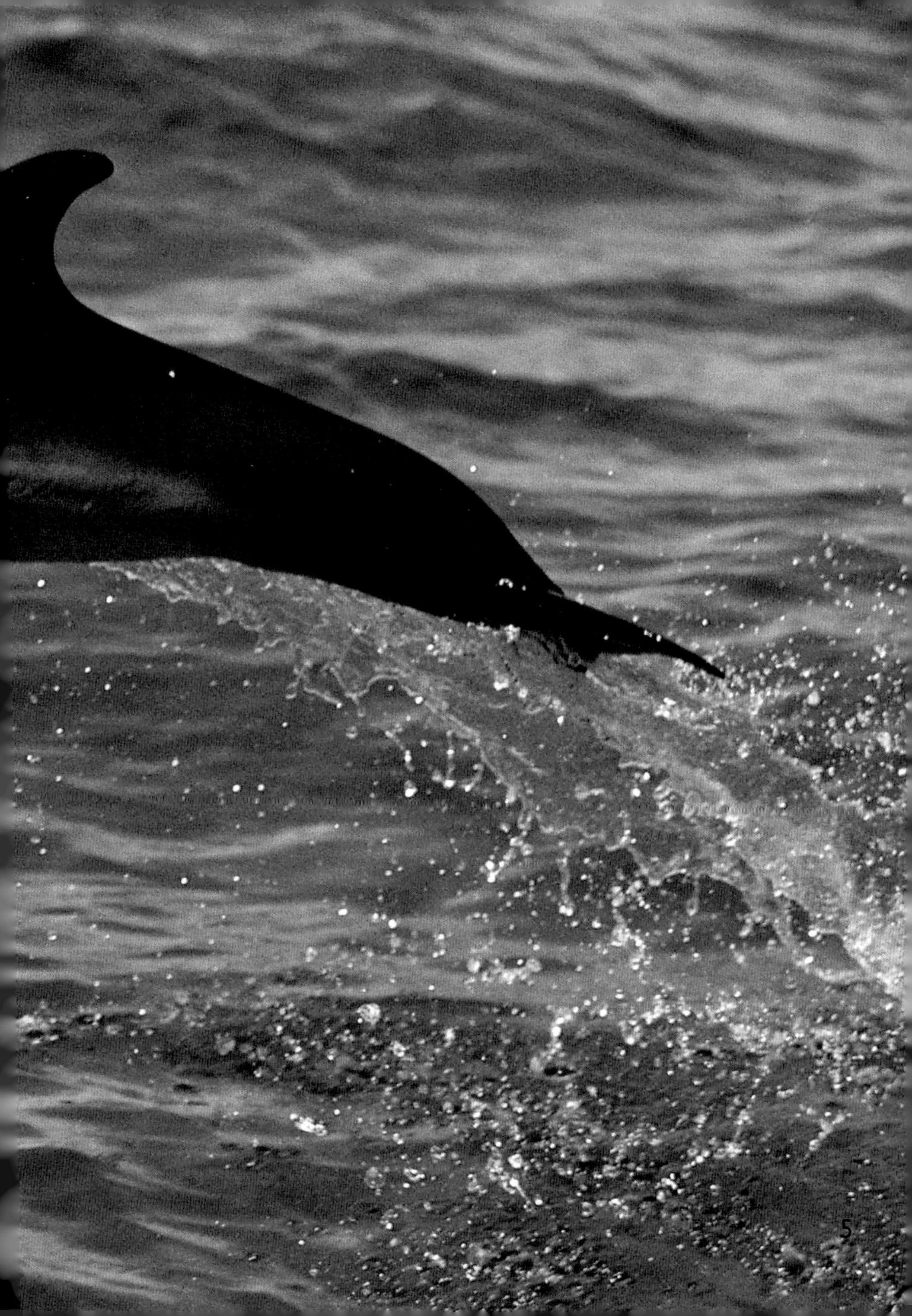

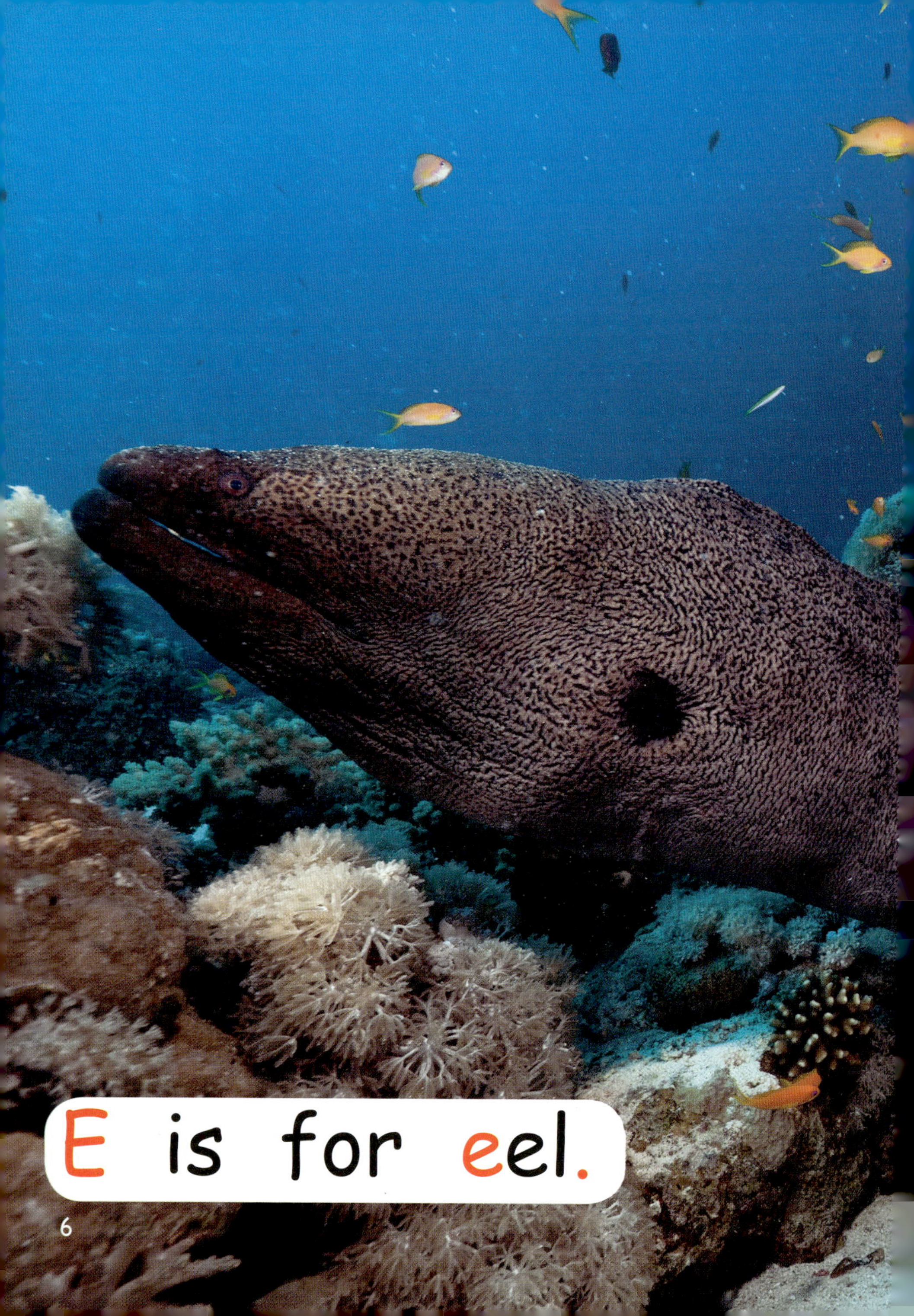

E is for eel.

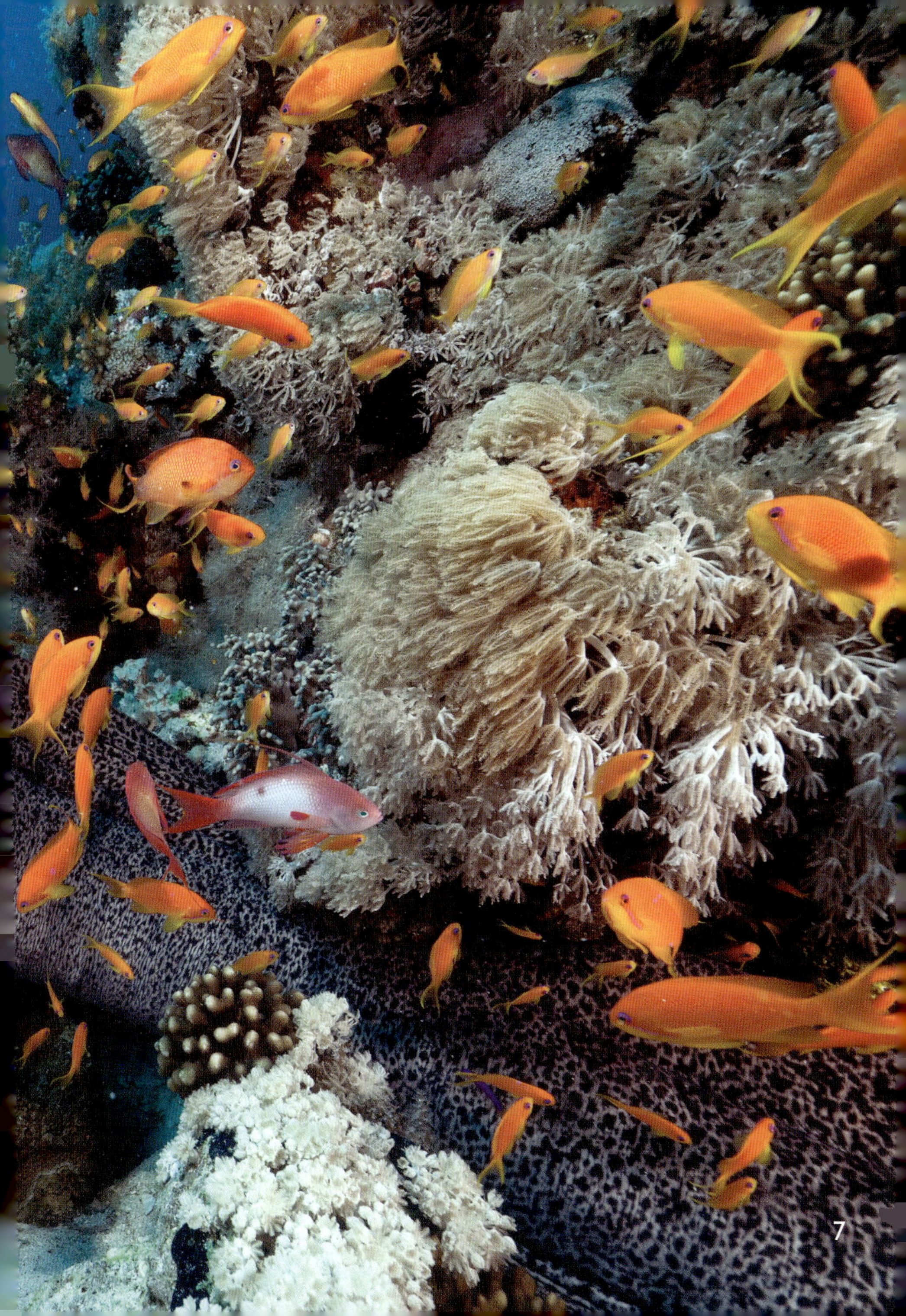

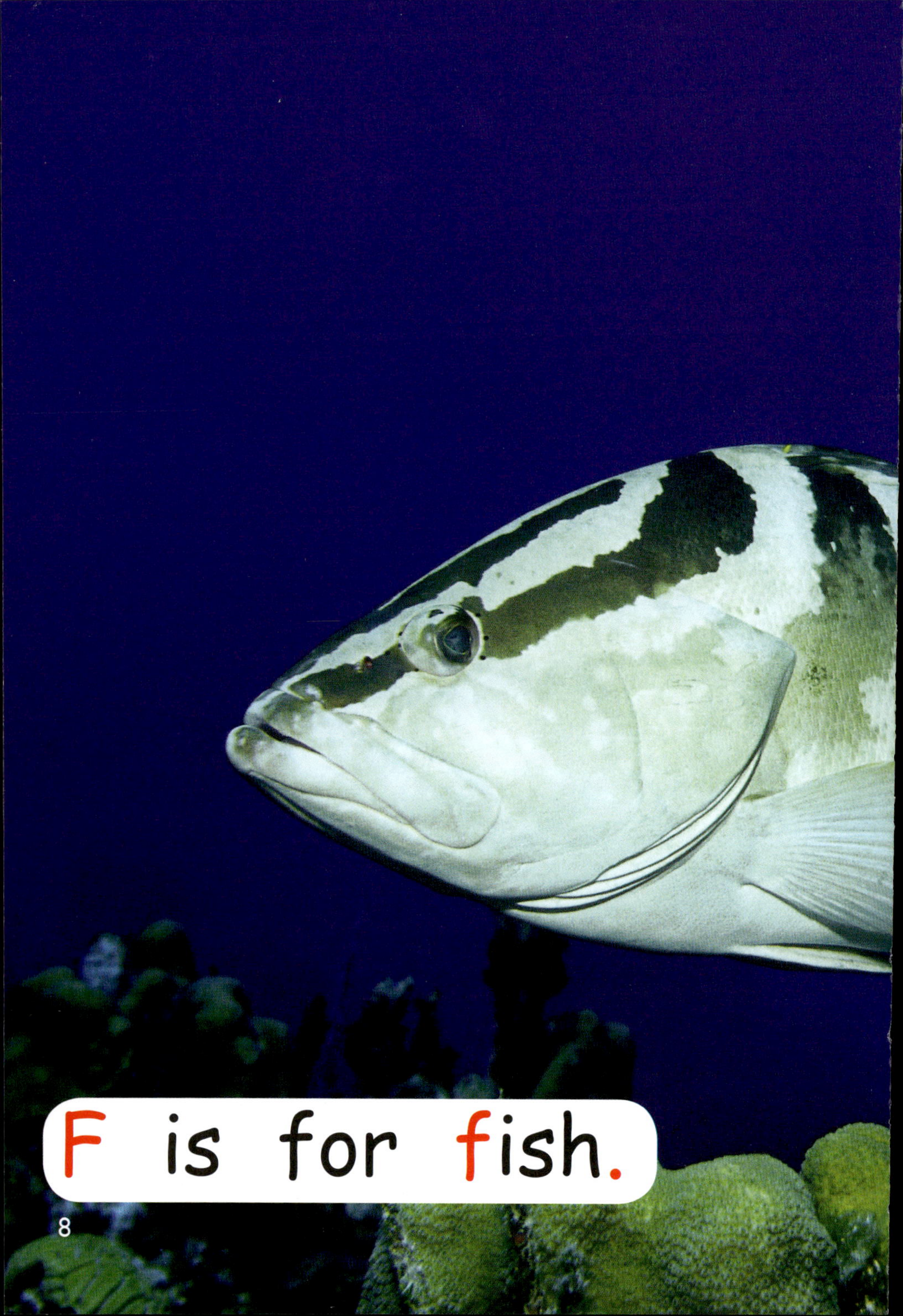

F is for fish.

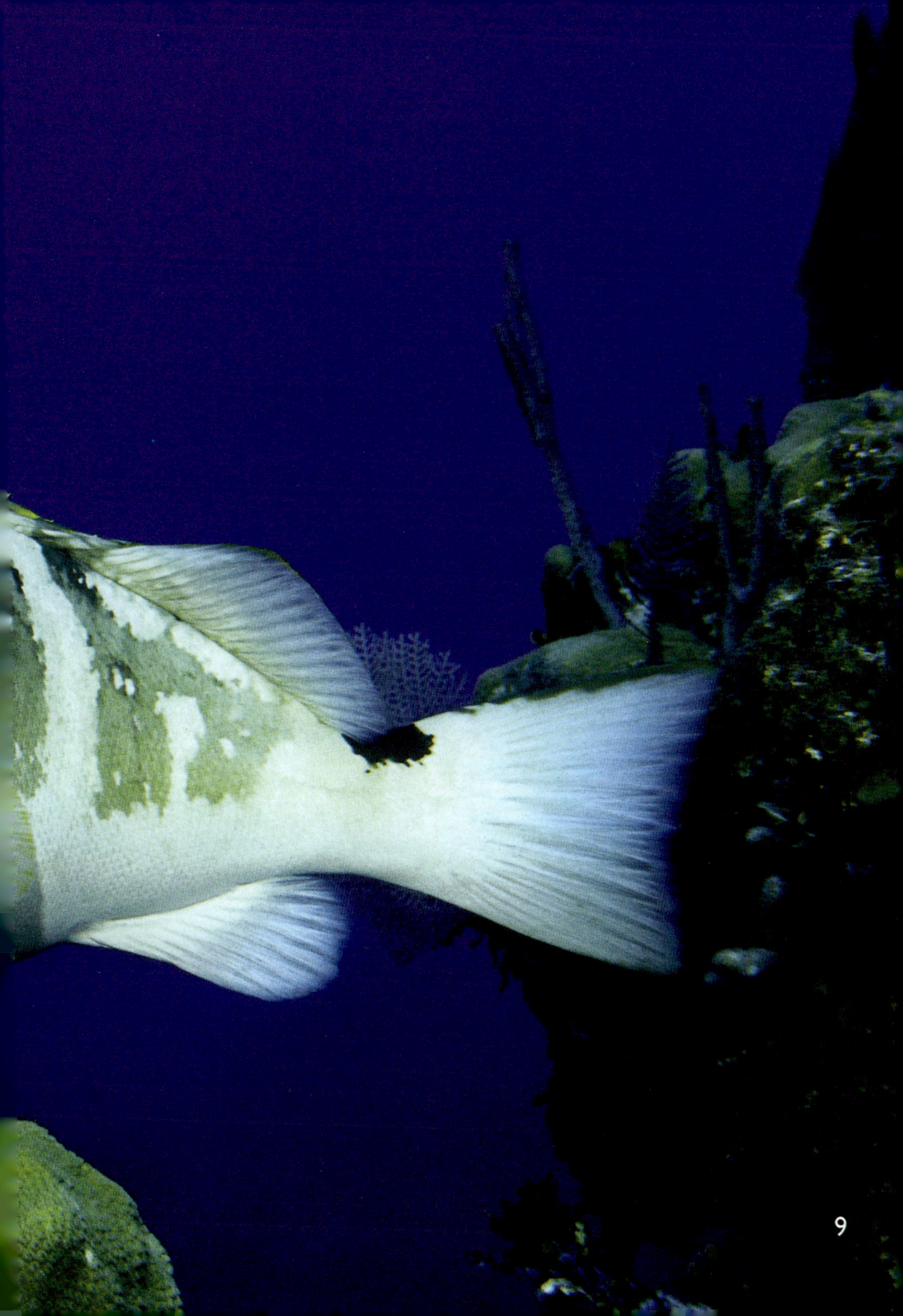

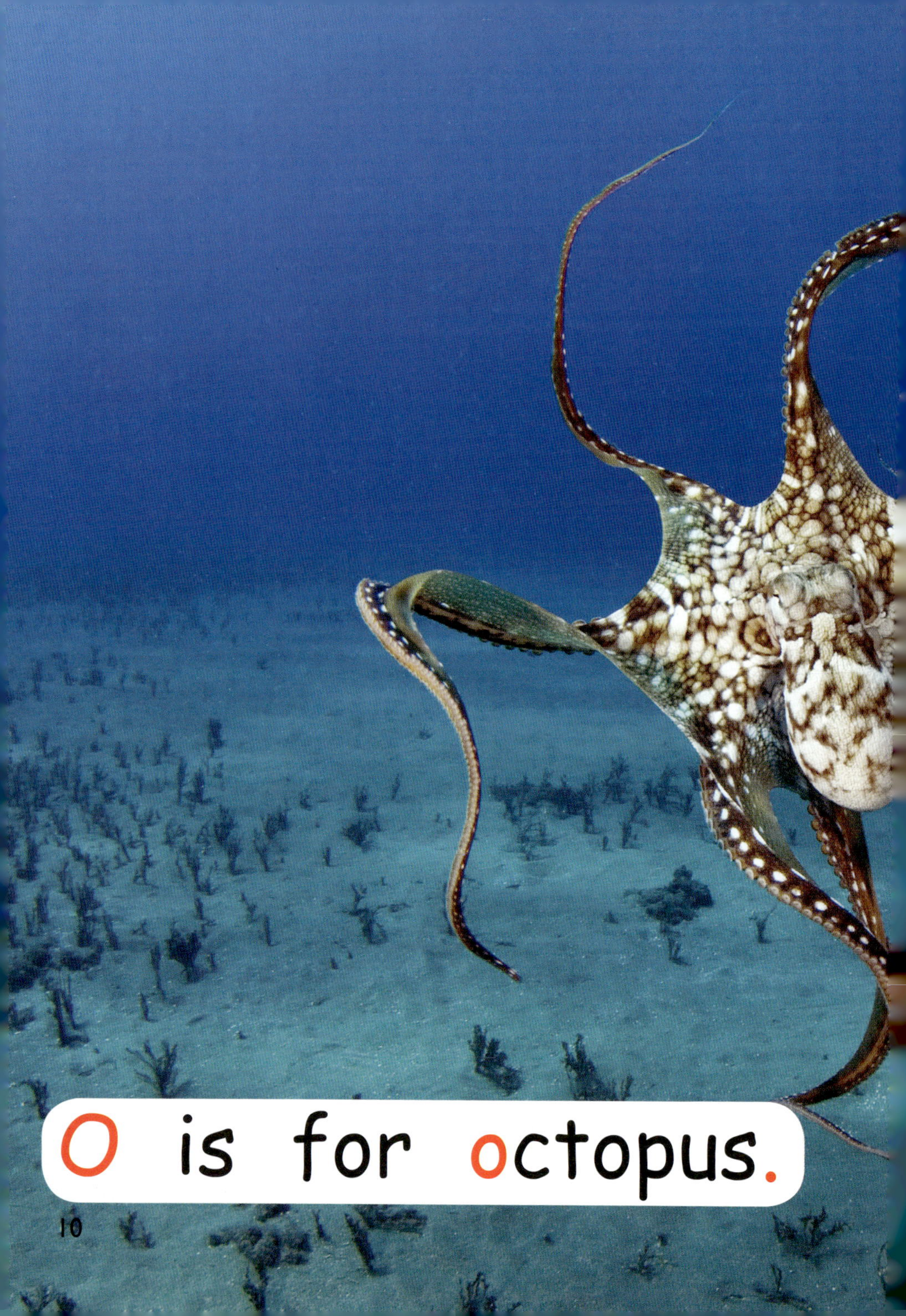

O is for octopus.

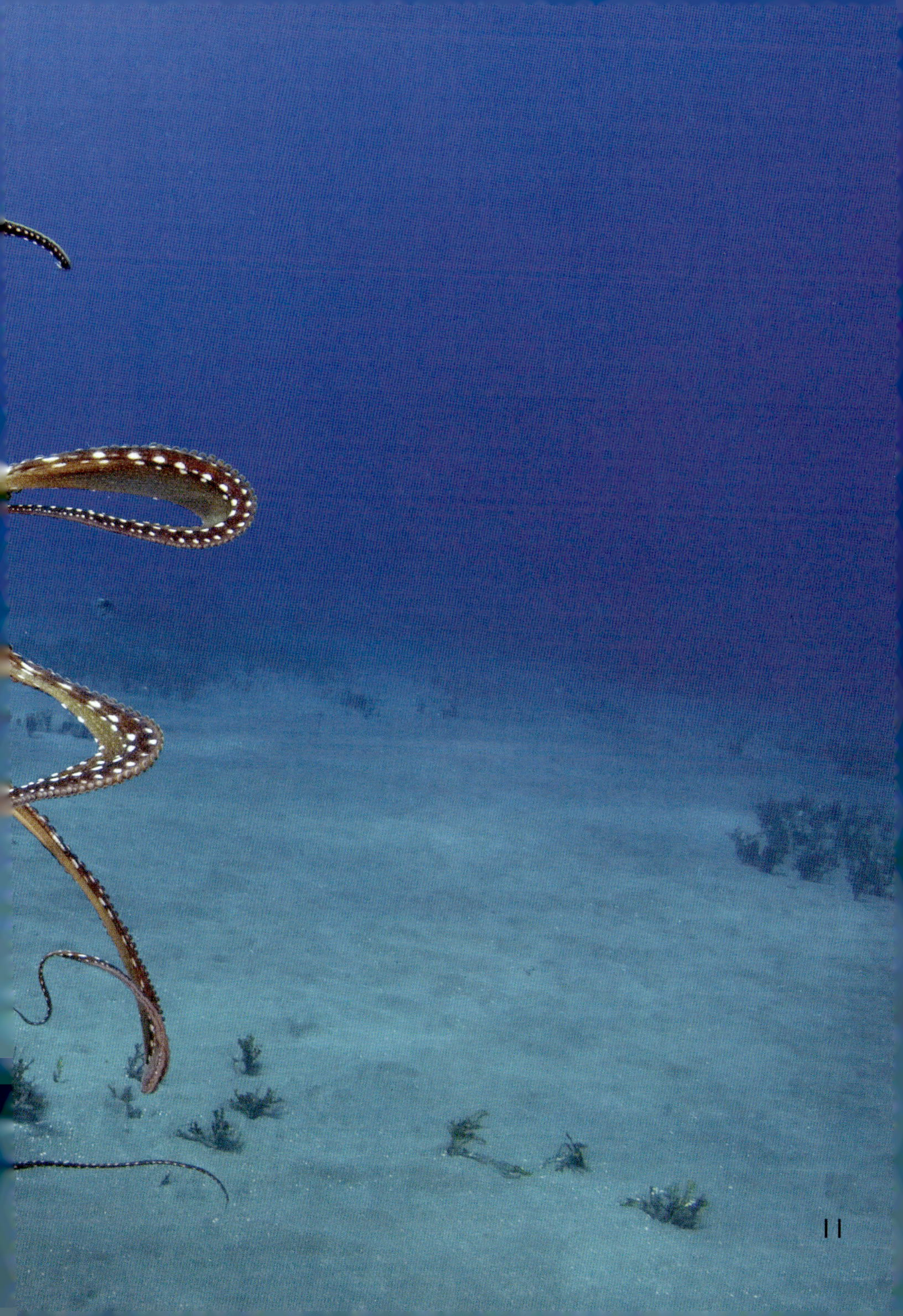

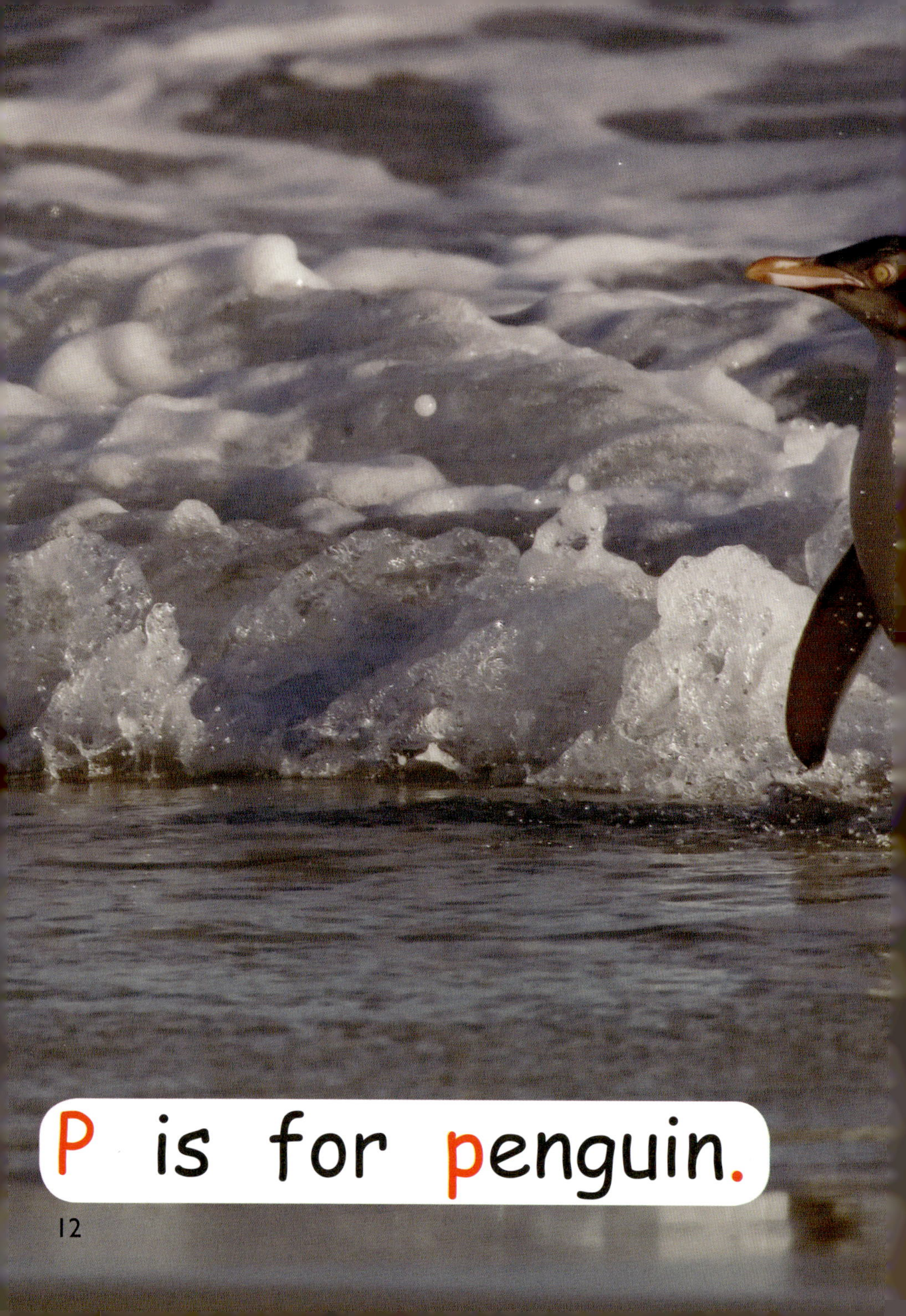

P is for penguin.

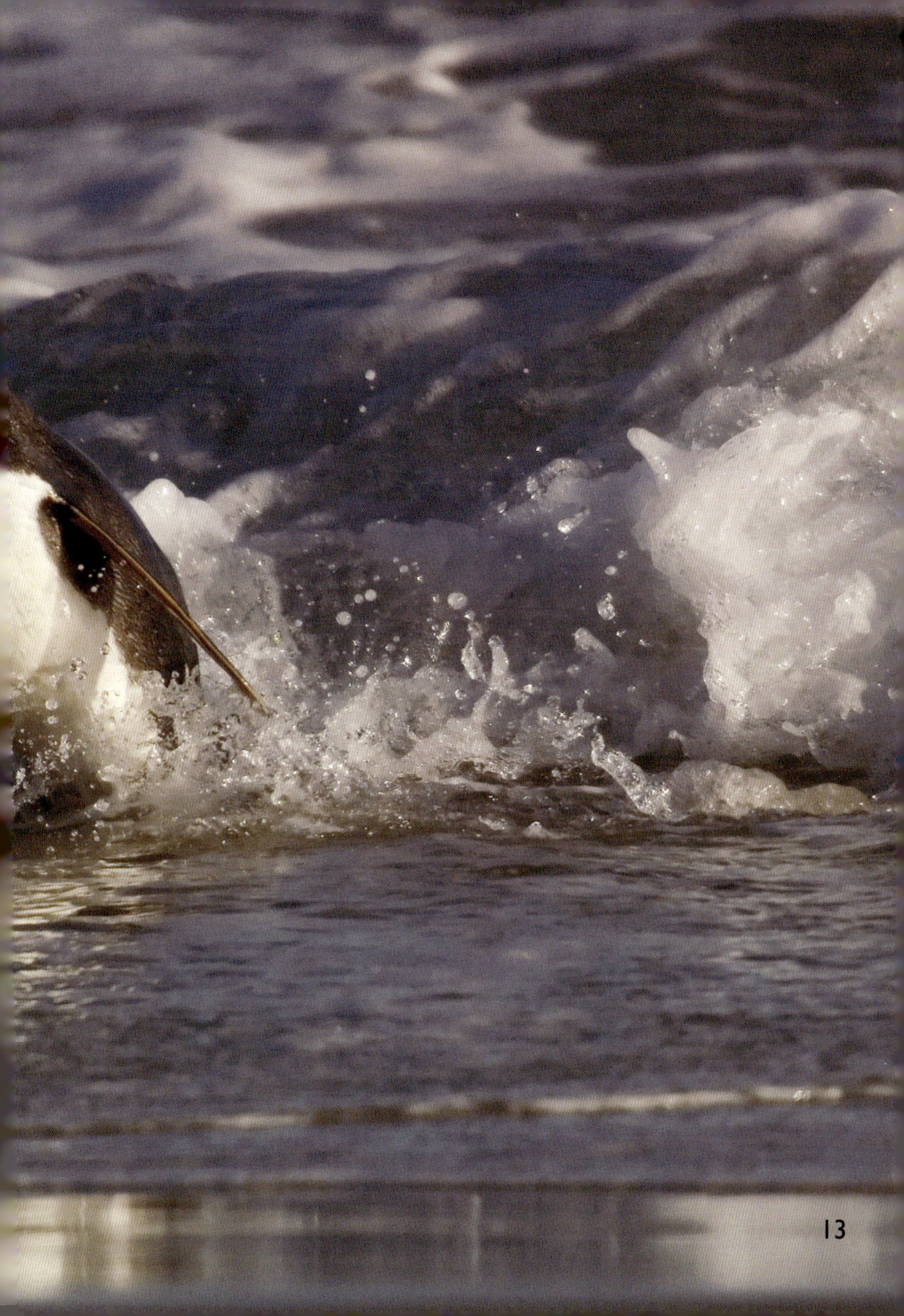

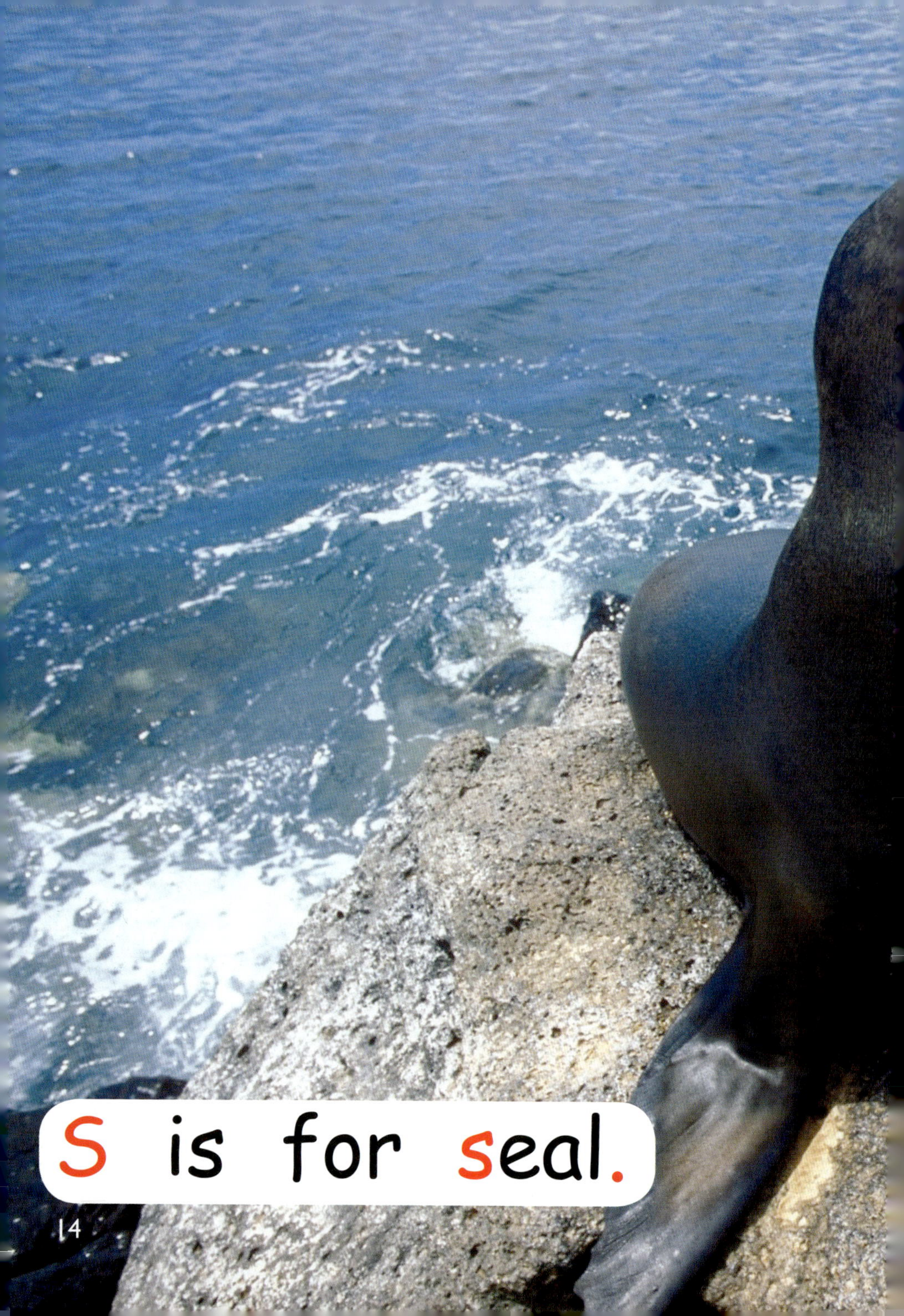

S is for seal.

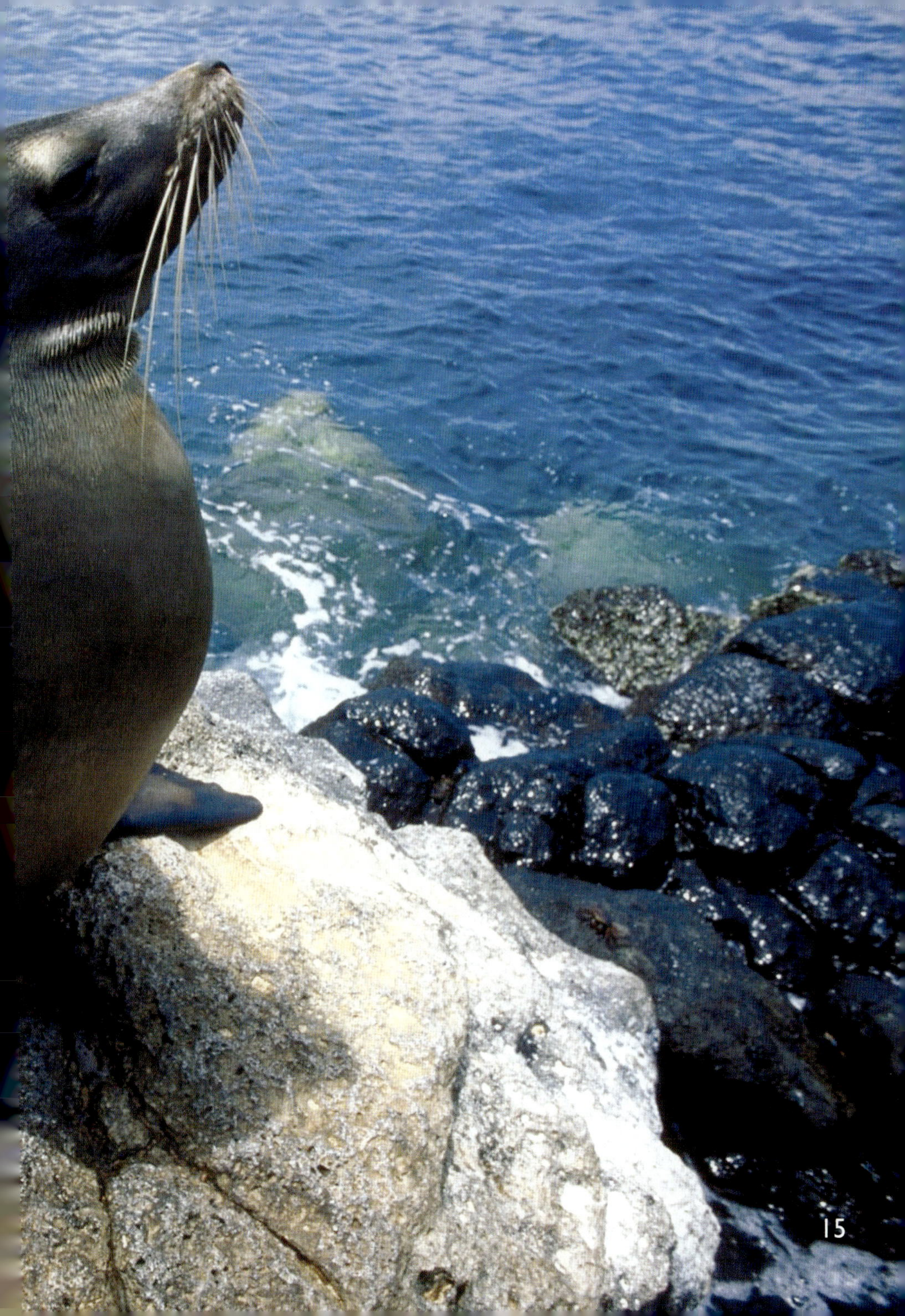

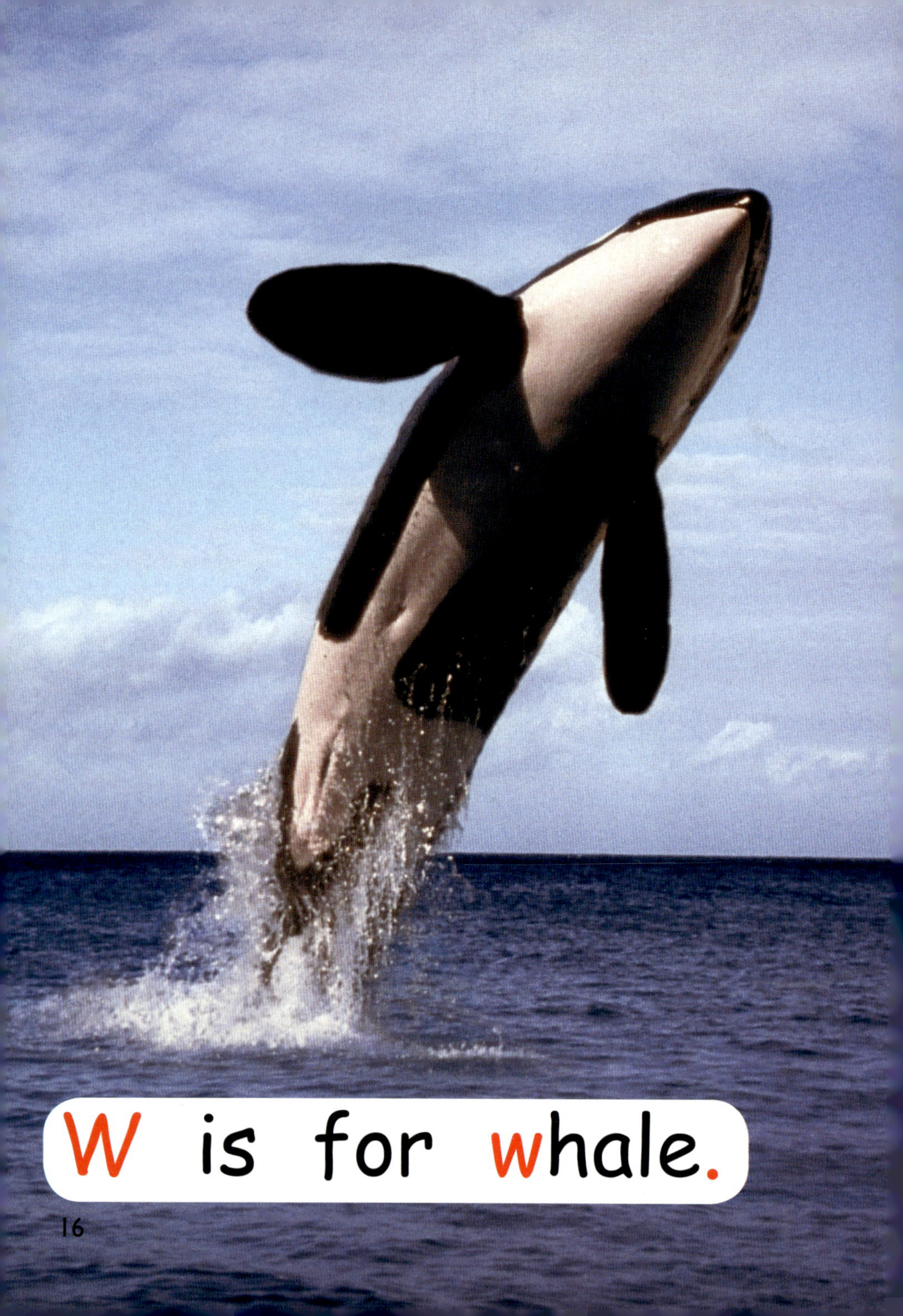

W is for whale.